Living in History

English homes through time captured with a
Gentle Twist to Perspective

Eli Ofir

Historical research:
Rosalind Chislett & Jane Davidson

England 2012

Living in History

Second Edition 2012

Published by Home Portraits 4 U Ltd.
www.homeportraits4u.co.uk

© Eli Ofir

Format and typeset by Design to Print UK Ltd.
www.designtoprintuk.com

Layout & cover graphic design:
Michal Guy, Tal Ofir, Eli Ofir and Rob Dewhurst

ISBN : 978-0-9568077-2-4

Printed and bound in India by Replika Press Pvt. Ltd.

This book is dedicated with all my love to Katia, my teacher for life, who opened my eyes to the light. Without her I would still be in total darkness.

Thank you Katia for helping me rediscover my love of drawing and for connecting me to this unique and deep expression of my God-given talent. I feel greatly honoured to have received this gift and I am full of joy and happiness that you opened my heart to share this gift with others through my drawings, and through this book. I feel so thankful and privileged to be able to bring these magnificent old English houses back to life.

Eli Ofir

Table of Contents

' ...and out of the strong came forth sweetness...'
(The Bible, Judges, Chapter 14/14)

Once upon a time there was a 14 year old boy who couldn't sit still for a minute. All day long he was playing ball in the school yard, dancing to rock 'n roll music, strumming his guitar, running, climbing and swimming in the sea.

He couldn't concentrate on anything that wasn't tangible or physically in front of him. This, of course, included his school work. There was no common ground between his visual and emotional worlds and school books, exams and times tables.

There was one thing though that connected the boy's heart to the outside world, something magical. He loved to draw. He'd never really learned how to draw, but ever since he could remember he'd drawn imaginary figures and scenes from distant lands and fantasy worlds, such as kings, castles, princesses, dragons, warriors and fairies.

Unfortunately, drawing kings and castles was not part of his school's curriculum. This made it difficult for the boy to express himself except through drawing on tables and chairs during lessons. These were his canvases. Unsurprisingly he frequently ended up in the headmaster's office, awaiting his weekly punishment...or just a telling off if he was lucky.

One Spring morning, in yet another boring literature lesson, the boy was scribbling away on the table in front of him, concentrating on the mysterious figure taking shape under his pen. It was a man crawling on all fours, bleeding, with torn clothes, with his hand stretched out in front of him as if he was trying to reach out for help. The boy was so focused on the figure he didn't notice a shadow looming above him.

"What are you doing young man?" yelled a familiar voice.

The shocked boy tried to hide his drawing with his hands, but with no great success as it covered more than half the table.

"Let me see what masterpiece you've created here today..." continued the voice sternly.

The boy didn't even look up. He was already planning the excuse he'd be telling the headmaster in a few minutes time...and planning what he would be doing for the rest of his day after he was thrown out of school. He slowly moved his hands away from the drawing.

There was silence. The air in the classroom was still. Nobody moved and nothing was heard from his teacher, not even the slightest groan or angry grunt. The boy lifted his eyes slowly upwards. His teacher was staring at his drawing as if there was no one else around, let alone 43 pupils waiting for her to continue with her lesson. She was totally engaged with the bleeding figure on all fours, crawling its way to the edge of the table.

The boy noticed that his teacher was holding a book of poems by Yehuda Amichai. Her finger was on the page she'd just been reading out to the class before she'd been interrupted by the budding artist.

"What have you drawn here?" she asked after what felt like an eternity.

"Nothing...just a man...I don't know...I'm sorry...' replied the boy nervously.

"Don't be sorry," said the teacher. "Just tell me what you were thinking when you drew this figure."

The boy noticed that the teacher's voice had changed. To his amazement it was now soft and tender. "..The man is injured and…he's trying to reach a place where he can get help," he replied.

"What's he feeling?"

"He's angry," answered the boy quietly.

The teacher looked at him with a compassionate, motherly gaze. The boy was alarmed – she must have gone completely crazy! The teacher, however, opened her book very slowly and, looking straight into his eyes, began reading out the poem she'd been reading to the class a few moments before.

"…and on grownups he has no pity at all,
He leaves them alone,
And sometimes they must crawl on all fours
In the burning sand
To reach the first-aid station
Covered with blood…"

The boy was in shock, realising he'd unconsciously drawn a scene from the poem. 'OK, nice one,' he thought. '…so maybe it won't be the headmaster today…I wonder what kind of punishment the teacher will give me instead.'

"Young man," said the teacher. "From this moment onwards…'

'Here it comes', laughed the boy in his mind.

"…you will not participate in writing in any of my classes and exams…"

'Wow! That's a new one', thought the boy.

"…instead you will only…draw!"

The boy's jaw dropped. 'What?! I must have missed something here…' he thought in astonishment.

The teacher continued, her voice warm and soft: "From now on in all my literature lessons you can draw whatever you feel like drawing," she said. "Just please bring a sketch book and some pens and pencils with you next time – I don't want to fund these tables from my own money!"

The boy couldn't grasp the magnitude of what had just happened. For the first time in his life someone had seen his potential and the inner beauty and creativity that was his natural gift. He didn't realise it yet, but this teacher had poured the first drop of water onto the seed of talent God had planted in him, the seed that was to blossom into the realisation of his true potential.

Mrs Dvora Silverstone

The teacher's name is Mrs Dvora Silverstone. This wonderful woman was brave enough to act outside the strict guidelines of the school and so she succeeded where others had failed. She recognised the thin line connecting my inner world and the world outside. She discovered the language I needed to express myself and grow to fulfil my destiny.

Mrs Silverstone, I thank you from the bottom of my heart. You were the first person to acknowledge my strength and open my heart to see my talent. The story I have just told changed my life. I will never forget your belief in me and the sensitivity and patience you had with me.

During my subsequent 20 year career as a hi-tech entrepreneur, my creativity and artistic skills were always at the core of my work. I was involved with companies that developed multimedia systems combining graphics, animation and visual interfaces. I was able to harness my artistic gift into practical business…just as Mrs Silverstone had helped me to do back at school.

One day I invited Mrs Silverstone to visit me at one of my companies, so she could see for herself what had grown from the seed she'd nurtured. It was a very emotional and loving visit.

At one point she took a piece of paper out of her purse. It was one of the original drawings of the bleeding man I had drawn 20 years before. She told me she'd met the poet Yehuda Amichai and showed him the drawing and told him the whole story. She said he'd been overwhelmed.

I will never forget my wonderful literature teacher sitting on my manager's office sofa that day. It was a complete closure for me.

Mr Meir Apelbaum

There is one other person who contributed significantly to my artistic career. His name was Mr Meir Apelbaum.

Meir was a lonely old Russian artist who I met through my school community activities when I was 15 years old. I visited him twice a week for many years and during those visits he taught me some basic drawing techniques, perspective and pen work.

I still have one of his sketches hanging on the wall in my house today. It's a picture of a wooden house in Siberia that he drew when he was prisoner there in the Second World War.

Meir's art work had a huge impact on me and I was deeply inspired by him. As time passed my family and I adopted him as a grandfather figure and we were close to him until he passed away 20 years later.

Thank you Meir for all you taught me with so much love.

Living in history

I become very emotional when I draw beautiful old houses. They are living history scattered everywhere across the English countryside. Driving along narrow country roads you can be sure that nearly every driveway you pass ends with a beautiful house with a history all of its own.

When I'm drawing a house, the fine detail of my pen work takes me on a magical journey where the history of each property is revealed with every brick and stone I immortalise.

The uneven lines of the roof, walls and beams deepen this mystery. That's why I slightly enhance these elements to bring out the warmth and personality of the houses. This Gentle Twist to Perspective is my unique style and my artistic signature. It transforms a house into a work of art that tells an ancient story.

I always draw with a free hand and never use a ruler. I use pen and ink and soft pencil and then smudge the pencil to shade some areas. I never use colour as I believe black and white brings a house to life more than colour ever will.

My passion for old and magnificent houses grows by the day. It's fascinating to realise that – whether a person lives in an end-of-terrace, semi-detached, detached or a manor house – they are literally living in history.

This is why I do my best to visit every house I draw and take photos and get a feel for its personality. I love to meet owners and hear their stories about their house and its history. If a house is too far away for me to visit I ask the owners to take photos from as many angles as possible. This gives me a good feel for their home and, most importantly, the way they feel about it.

Original drawings and stationary prints

The majority of properties I work with have lots of interesting angles to draw from so many clients commission drawings from two or more elevations. Sometimes I draw three, four or even five original portraits of the same house.

After I finish my drawings I scan them digitally in high resolution onto a CD so that as well as having an original work of art owners can print off letterheads, greeting cards, placemats and any other stationary prints they desire.

Full circle

Over the years I have drawn hundreds of beautiful houses for many different clients. I'm so grateful for this privilege.

When I looked through my portfolio recently I had the idea of illustrating the historical evolution of English architecture through my drawings. I made contact with Ros and Jane, both very experienced house historians, and together we came up with the fascinating journey you see in this book. I hope we have done justice to the truly magical beauty of English homes.

I feel humble and grateful that I am blessed with this talent for drawing and that I am able to pass on this heavenly gift and touch the hearts of others. I can say with pride that I have finally returned to my roots, when I was a little boy drawing on a classroom table so long ago…

…once again I am drawing castles in the land of kings and princesses.

Eli Ofir

A brief history of English architecture

English architecture did not follow a rigid timeline with clear divisions between periods and styles of building. Many stages overlapped and many styles may well have been in use in the same region or even in the same building concurrently. The majority of the houses in this book are in the south east of England, an area frequently in the forefront of design innovation

This book contains portraits of different types of buildings; not only houses but also pubs, colleges and converted agricultural buildings. They date from diverse periods in history and feature varied construction materials, for example timber-framing with flint, handmade bricks and later mass produced materials. Inevitably the number of alterations to the original construction increase with the age of a house.

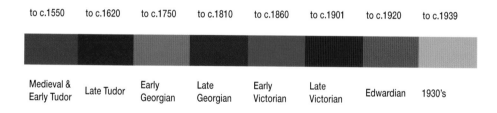

to c.1550	to c.1620	to c.1750	to c.1810	to c.1860	to c.1901	to c.1920	to c.1939
Medieval & Early Tudor	Late Tudor	Early Georgian	Late Georgian	Early Victorian	Late Victorian	Edwardian	1930's

Establishing the date of any house of a significant age can be problematic. A precise date can only be obtained from surviving documentation or by using tree-ring dating on samples of the timber frame. The majority of written records have been lost, and deeds have been either superseded or filed and forgotten about in solicitors' offices or even destroyed. However, clues can be found via an analysis of style and construction, bearing in mind that these differed considerably from county to county.

Each house has a different history, some longer and more complex than others. The brief details in this book only hint at the full story of each house. Much more can be found out from a variety of sources. With luck and careful research it's possible to name all of the previous occupants, how long they lived there and what families they had. Archive records might also reveal who the builder was and when it was built.

Buildings often change their use over years. For example, oast houses can become habitable premises and primitive labourers' cottages can become desirable properties once they're extended.

The location of a house is important as it often explains why it came to be built there. Centres of villages sometimes move and towns grow away from their original centres for reasons such as geography or convenience. The arrival of the railways led to ribbon development on a significant scale.

This book is a celebration of houses cherished by owners who realise they'll only be passed on to future generations through careful maintenance. Each chapter shows examples of a particular time in English history. This is by no means exhaustive and not all phases are included. The explanation at the beginning of each chapter describes the influences of the period and how they were manifested in the architecture.

We're so lucky that it's still possible to walk down many English streets and identify a wide spectrum of buildings dating from medieval times onwards; buildings that still play a part in today's world.

The House Historians

Rosalind Chislett and Jane Davidson are graduates in Archaeology. They met at Kent University and decided to work together using their experience in architecture, archival research and genealogy to investigate house histories.

They founded House Historians in 2000 and have researched hundreds of houses, predominantly in the South East (in Kent and Sussex), although they can undertake commissions anywhere in England. Their background in archaeological research has been invaluable in the investigation of a wide range of properties from cottages to country houses.

Research for this book has meant condensing house histories into a few sentences, which at times has been frustrating, but perhaps owners will now be tempted to know more…

Rosalind Chislett BA Hons
Jane Davidson BA Hons

Medieval and Early Tudor

Medieval and early Tudor architecture (up to c.1550)

The earliest surviving houses in England date from the Medieval and early Tudor period, and these are only houses that belonged to the wealthier members of society.

Houses of the poor of the time were thrown up using locally obtained cheap or free materials, which is why they soon fell down again leaving little trace. Richer people could afford to use more durable fabrics and employ experienced builders, which inevitably led to a longer lifespan for their houses.

The Medieval period, also known as the Middle Ages, started with the reign of Edward the Confessor (1042-1066). Private housing changed little during this period. In fact it didn't start to significantly change until what is known as the Second Great Rebuilding at the beginning of the 16th century, during the reign of Henry VIII.

House building largely conformed to the standard pattern of each locality, with most innovations starting in the south east of England, where distinctive house types such as the Continuous Jetty and the Wealden came into being. The Norman Conquest also brought architectural influences from the French aristocracy, although this chiefly had an impact on the many castles and churches they built.

Design

The houses of the rich centred on great halls, open to the roof, where smoke from an open hearth gradually found its way out through gaps in the thatch, which was the most common type of roofing material at the time. The fire was used to heat the hall and to cook food suspended above it either in a cauldron or on a spit. Chimneys were inserted at a later date.

The fabric of the walls depended on what was readily available in the surrounding landscape and varied from stone to cob and flint, or most commonly, timber frame in-filled with wattle and daub.

The timber (usually oak) was cut and measured by the craftsman carpenter at his yard and pre-fabricated as the frame that would eventually be erected. To ensure the pieces were reassembled in the right order the carpenter carved marks in the timber based on forms of Roman numerals.

During its erection the frame was supported on temporary blocks that were later replaced by a stone or brick plinth. This kept the base above the damp of the earth. Deep foundations were considered unnecessary. Houses were built in a series of bays or sections without corridors so that the only access through rooms was by doors in the dividing walls.

Between the main timber supports, the wattle panels were oak staves inserted into beams interwoven with hazel withies. This basket-like finish was covered by the daub – a mixture of clay, dung and chopped straw. Finally, the walls were lime-washed or painted. If properly maintained this material lasted indefinitely, but when deterioration occurred the daub was replaced with other materials, such as stone and brick.

The exterior of early timber-framed houses displayed large panels with curved cross braces to hold the structure stable. Later on close studded timbers, an expensive process, displayed the wealth of owners.

Windows were very small, if they existed at all, to avoid drafts. Sometimes they had a wooden shutter that could be closed at night and during bad weather. Doors were simple constructions made of planks. This meant the atmosphere inside these houses was very dark and smoky.

Only the very grandest houses had any durable floor covering, such as tile. Most had rushes covering a consolidated earth floor, which had to be regularly renewed. In some areas of the country the hall was situated at a first floor level with livestock quartered below. This kept cattle and sheep safe and also provided a form of central heating from their bodies. Access to the upper living quarters was often by external steps.

Privacy

There was very little privacy for most people at this time. However, yeomen and their families were lucky enough to have an area at the end of the hall, cut off from the general public. This was their private quarters or solar. This space was often divided into an upper and lower level with a simple ladder for access to the floor above. The lower level could be a sitting room or bedroom, while the upper floor housed storage space or an additional sleeping area.

There was also a division for eating arrangements. Although everybody ate in the same space, owners sat on a raised dais in the upper or solar end of the hall. Fixed benches were provided to receive guests and trestle tables were added when meals were served.

There was frequently another section at the other end of the hall – the service area which housed small rooms such as a buttery, a brewhouse or a milkhouse, where food preparation and storage took place.

Above these spaces was storage for household goods or sacks of produce such as wheat. There was sometimes a cross passage between the service rooms and the hall so that servants could move from the front to the rear of the house without disturbing the yeoman and his guests.

Town houses

Houses in towns differed to some degree from houses of a similar size in the country. They were crowded closer together and, because the predominant material was wood, there were often fires.

For this reason King Richard I passed a law requiring the lower parts of town houses to be made of stone or brick. This brick was often accompanied by a jetty at the first floor level, which produced an overhung first floor.

There has been considerable speculation about the purpose of these jetties. They certainly protected lower walls from the weather in the absence of gutters and provided more floor space on the upper storey. They may also have been created because of problems of obtaining posts long enough to run the full height of buildings. The most plausible reason for them, however, seems to be one of fashion, as they are almost always found on the front of the house, even when the prevailing wind is at the rear.

If owned by a tradesman, town houses were habitually built side-on to the street. This allowed space for a hall and service quarters to the rear. The front became a shop section to display wares. Storage areas were created beneath ground level, which had the added advantage of keeping goods cool.

Inns

Surprisingly many inns have survived from the Middle Ages. They originated in two ways; first as an alehouse or tavern selling beer and other drinks, and second as a hostel for travellers.

Both had connections with the local Church. It was common for Churches to supplement their income by brewing and selling ale from booths in the churchyard and later from a Church House nearby. The alehouse could also be a sideline for a farmer or some other tradesman. It is therefore not always easy to determine whether a building was originally a pub or a private house.

Luxury items

Furniture and household goods were very simple and few, but with the steady growth in the middle classes, especially successful traders, the demand for luxury items grew over the years.

Previously, for example, roof frameworks were constructed from huge but plain timbers. Now elaborate carvings were added to the central supporting crown post, as well as ornate mouldings on other load bearing timbers.

This era saw times of prosperity and famine, the Black Death, wars with Europe and civil unrest during the Wars of the Roses, culminating in the reign of the first Tudor ruler Henry VII. It is a credit to the builders that houses from this period have survived until today, albeit adapted to a lesser or greater degree by succeeding generations.

J.D.

Medieval and Early Tudor

A word from the current owner:

When we first looked at the house we loved it immediately. Nothing was straight and all the floors sloped, as you'd expect in a house that's over 500 years old. It was clear it needed some tender loving care, but it was a great example of a Wealden Hall House. The house was a grain store in Victorian times; we still find small amounts of grain in nooks and crannies. We also found, when renovating, a small compartment hidden in a beam with a bag of low value old coins in it. This is the house's lucky money – coins hidden by past owners over several hundred years to give them and the house good fortune. We added a few coins to the bag and returned it to its hiding place. The house has a very friendly and protective atmosphere, perhaps because it's given so many people a home for so long. We are very happy here. home for so long. We are very happy here.

"My Gentle Twist to Perspective came very handy in this drawing. The original wooden beams have such a strong contrast that it came naturally to me to have them move from the centre outwards in a delicate and quirky way. This is one of my favourite drawings"

This spectacular timber-framed house is known as a Wealden Hall house. Believed to have been built in 1493, the exterior retains much of its original structure and appears to have changed little from that time. The framing has plaster infilling and a plain tile roof although the steep pitch may indicate it was originally thatched. In addition, mortices on the right hand side of the left door show where there was once a two storey bay window. Both end bays have fine surviving jetties to the front and side supported on moulded dragon posts. The multiple brick ridge stack indicates where the chimney breast was inserted after open halls went out of fashion.

The house was once part of a larger estate owned by the Filmer family who were prominent in Elizabethan times. The estate was broken up and the house was sold in 1916 after the main heir, Sir Robert, died on active service in France during the First World War. A previous Sir Robert Filmer was a friend of Charles I during the Civil War. He was imprisoned in Leeds Castle and his Manor House was sacked ten times by the parliamentarians. It is now a prison.

Medieval and Early Tudor

"This is one of the first houses I drew on commission in England. Although it's been in my portfolio for a long time I still use it as one of the best examples of my work. For years I had this portrait on the front page on my leaflets and web pages. Its composition and quirkiness just make it perfect. It has helped sell my work ever since. It will always have a special place in my heart.."

This Grade II listed property was built in the fourteenth century. The house is timber-framed with a Horsham slab roof, half hipped to the right. It was originally built as a Hall House, with a later addition of a fine pair seventeenth century ridged chimney stacks with mouldings to the top and bottom. It has a Tudor stone fireplace with a brick flue in the deep fireplace, with moulded spandrels and the date 1597 carved on the lintel.

One of the earliest documents relating to the house is dated 1633. A flagpole that flew the Royal Standard at Elizabeth II's coronation stood in the garden. The house was also once used as recording studio, where many artists including Vanessa Mae and the Happy Mondays recorded albums.

Medieval and Early Tudor

"This close studded timber-frame house is so classic it looks as if it's just popped out of an old history book. The black and white contrasting stripes give it a Zebra look. Being a court shape it was difficult for me to find the right angle to draw. Finally, I decided on this elevation, which to my eyes is the one that best reflects its beauty."

This magnificent house in the heart of the Weald of Kent is listed as Grade II* with good reason. Its earliest part dates from the 1400s when it was an open Hall House. This style took its name from the central hall where the greater part of family life took place. This section has larger square framing complete with Kentish tension bracing.

In the 16th century a north wing and cottage extension were added with distinctive close studded timber-framing and jetties on three sides. This necessitated the use of dragon beams with brackets to support the diagonal floor joists. The building has examples of very early window glass.

The house is thought to have been built by a forge master at the peak of the iron industry that once dominated the region. Much later, during the 20th century, it was owned by the Letts family of diary fame.

Medieval and Early Tudor

"This is one of the most classical old houses I have come across. It has lots of character and is beautiful from all angles. Its surroundings are also breathtaking – it's in the middle of a wood with deer and pheasants running all around. It's a magical place."

This Grade II listed building was built in the sixteenth century. It is a two storey timber-framed house and the ground floor has red brick infill. The roof is tile hung and there are casement windows.

Medieval and Early Tudor

"This is one of the oldest houses I've drawn. When I first saw it I had the feeling of going back in time. It is very well preserved and it feels as if it has been given lots of love from its owners over the years. I feel as if I know every brick in the house after drawing it."

The first documents relating to this early medieval Hall House, a yeoman's farmhouse, are from 1356. The house was situated in a large enclosure. The original builder was a moderately wealthy man and he displayed his wealth with an upper storey jetty.

The house was built of local stone in coursed rubble with window facings in Bath stone.

The interior ground floors were laid with oak. In 1697, the farm had a total of 15 acres. In 1839, it was sold to William Leveson Gower of Titsey Place and became part of a large estate.

Palaeolithic implements have been found in the grounds. They consist of 34 hand axes and eight Flakes. The flakes are in the Pitt Rivers Museum, Oxford.

Medieval and Early Tudor

"One of my first commissions in England, this well known inn is situated in the middle of Ashdown Forest not far from where I live. I go there often and I am proud of my portrait hanging on the wall. I've also seen some Christmas cards and brochures printed with the portrait on them. It's a lovely old place with great food…"

This Grade II listed building was originally a row of three cottages and dates back to 1430. The building is covered in weather boarding and has a half hipped roof. There are casement windows which, on the first floor, have diamond shaped glass panes.

It was not until the eighteenth century that the cottages became an inn. It is claimed that the inn was a haunt for smugglers, with rum their speciality. The Hatch Inn is situated in the heart of Ashdown forest, close to the Winnie-the-Pooh Bridge.

Medieval and Early Tudor

A word from the current owner:

When we first viewed the property it was in need of a great deal of renovation. In fact it took five years to completely renovate it, and nine months before we could live in it at all. It's a house with a lot of character. Our biggest surprise was returning home one day to find a digger, which had been taking out part of the back garden to stop the dampness in the wall, perched precariously on what turned out to be an original well. This well is now a feature of the garden. Our daughter had great fun having friends around for house and garden parties.

As we've opened up more of the house we've found various china jugs from the past, which were covered over when cupboards were put in. We are quite sure that there are still some secrets hidden in this old cottage waiting to be explored.

"Flint is very powerful to draw by hand in terms of movement and contrast. I love this portrait especially because of the flint and brickwork combination. The angle of the main portrait has a very strong perspective that gives deep feeling to the drawing. It's one of my favourites."

This Grade II listed property is medieval in origin and was formerly divided into several cottages. The left range was added in the late seventeenth century. The building is timber-framed with flint and brick infill. The interior has a central cruck truss with blades terminating above the collar. There's one other cruck blade to the rear, between the right bays.

Between the cruck trusses is a timber-framed cross wall, possibly a spere truss, with curved brace and tie beam notched to carry the purlin. The house was reconstructed in the nineteenth century, and refurbished in the 1980s, and is now a single dwelling. It was the premises of the local blacksmith for many centuries. The blacksmith's workshop is situated in the garden.

LateTudor

Late Tudor architecture (approx 1551-1620)

Comparative peace under the Tudor monarchs brought prosperity to England. The decline of private castles and defensive architecture, and its replacement by country houses, was one of the great achievements of the Tudor age.

The 16th century was a period of extraordinary building activity. The era heralded a passion for tearing down old houses and building anew. From courtiers to yeoman and cottagers, homeowners were yearning for improvements. There was a growing emphasis on domestic comfort and general living standards at all levels of society improved. This building boom has been called the Great Rebuilding.

The swelling ranks of skilled craftsmen enabled the construction of great numbers of well built houses. Architecture became a talking point and a symbol of status and social rivalry. The common theme that characterises this period was a growing awareness of architecture as an art form capable of intellectual analysis and appreciation. The dissolution of the monasteries provided surplus land as well as a source of stone and other building materials. The evidence of this architectural boom is still visible throughout England.

The style of houses moved away from defensive architecture, for example moated manor houses, and started to be more based on aesthetics. Quadrangular, H or E-shaped plans became more common.

The majority of houses were built from local materials, timber, brick or stone. The difficulty and expense of transporting building materials meant that all but the most extravagant builders were restricted to local sources. Stone and timber were the most popular materials, while brick denoted higher status throughout the country.
It was also fashionable for buildings to incorporate devices, or riddles, which served to demonstrate the owners' wit and to delight visitors. A desire for their names to live on after their death led to owners having a wealth of initials, dates and heraldic devices emblazoned on buildings.
The four centred arch, now known as the Tudor arch, was also a defining feature. And some of the most remarkable oriel windows belong to this period, where mouldings are more spread out and the foliage becomes more naturalistic.

Italian and Flemish influence

During the reigns of Henry V111 and Edward V1, many Italian artists came over to England and built with various decorative features. Later in the century, Flemish craftsmen succeeded these Italians.

The late Tudor period chimney stack and enclosed hearths resulted in the decline of the great hall based around the medieval open hearth. Instead, fireplaces could now be placed upstairs, and it became possible to have a second storey that ran the whole length of the house.

So the period from 1500-1530 marked the end of the open hall; houses after this date were built with first floor chambers above all the rooms and an enclosed fireplace. Tudor chimney pieces became large and elaborate to draw attention to the owner's adoption of this new technology, and the continuous jetty appeared as a way to show off the modernity of having a complete full length upper floor.

At the lower end of the social scale chimneys and glazed windows became part of more modest houses for the first time. Houses in general were becoming lighter and cleaner, with more private space, heating and better sanitation.
Within cities and towns, tall and narrow houses were constructed to make the most of the tightly packed space. Merchants and artisans built storey upon storey, generally living above their shops.
Timber-framing was still popular despite the fire risk. One advantage of this was that upper storeys could be jettied out over the street.

Elizabethan architecture

Elizabethan architecture is the name given to early Renaissance architecture in England during the reign of Queen Elizabeth 1. This style arrived in England after spreading through the Low Countries, where among other features it acquired versions of the Dutch gable. It was also at this time that English houses adopted the Asian concept of a long gallery as the chief reception room.

In England, the Renaissance tended to manifest itself in large square tall houses such as Longleat House. Often these buildings had asymmetrical towers that hint at the evolution from medieval fortified architecture.

Symmetrical plans were favoured, but otherwise the Renaissance influence appeared mainly in classical details, such as columns beside a door or fireplace, and round headed arches for front doors and niches, which could be shell shaped.

The Elizabethans delighted in glittering expanses of glazing, made possible by the new availability of cheaper glass. Interiors had elaborate fireplace surrounds, square panelling, friezes and ceilings decorated in strap-work.

Jacobean architecture

Elizabethan architecture was followed by houses built in the Jacobean style, an early phase of English Renaissance architecture. This style is named after King James I of England with whose reign it is associated.

Though the Jacobean period spanned only 22 years, it had a major impact on English domestic architecture. It was an exciting period of experiment and discovery that inspired an extraordinary range of architectural styles.

Although the general lines of Elizabethan design remained, there was more consistent application of formal design and the use of columns, pilasters, arcades and flat roofs.

Plain Classical formality coexisted with French, Italian and Dutch design, adapted to English tastes. This resulted in an explosion in new ideas and splendidly overblown ornament, which was described at the time as 'a heap of craziness of decorations... very disgusting to see'.

This flamboyant style also influenced furniture and decorative design.

Local materials

The majority of houses were still built of local materials. The precise material used was largely imposed by geological factors which gave rise to regional variations. The difficulty and expense of transporting materials from elsewhere meant that all but the most extravagant builders used materials from the surrounding areas.

Brick was used in prestigious buildings, but the majority of houses were built in stone. Finely dressed stone was indicative of social status and was prominently displayed on principal elevations.

In many counties oak timber-framing remained the main building material. Oak also continued to be used for interior fittings such as floorboards, doors and panelling. Some areas, for example Plymouth, experienced a shortage of timber due to the demands of the shipbuilding industry.

Tiles were the most popular roofing material and were produced locally. Slate roofing, which came mainly from Devon and Cornwall, was reserved for the wealthy. Horsham sandstone slate was very popular because it divided into thinner sections and provided a lighter roof covering. The blue slates of Wales were used on country houses and church buildings.

Lead was a highly expensive material and provided the only watertight covering. Thatching remained popular with smaller domestic buildings with chimneys and fireplaces commonplace. Mortar for binding stone and brick – generally composed of lime and sand with oyster shells – was added to make it damp resistant.

Iron was used for a variety of purposes, functional and decorative, such as clamps for stonework, glazing bars, nails, hinges and fire-backs. Glazed windows were found in the most modest of houses due to the considerable expansion of the glass making industry. Even so glass continued to be a highly valued material.

R.C.

Late Tudor

"This portrait was quite a challenge for me to draw. The house is extremely long and it took about five or six photos to cover it all. For the main angle I chose the view from the lake. I love this angle as it shows the house fading to the right while giving a glimpse of the beautiful gardens. "

Situated in the picturesque Mole Valley in Surrey, this extended farmhouse is at the centre of a 100 acre estate and is Grade II listed. It is timber-framed and in-filled with colour washed brick. The earliest part of this three sided property dates from the late 16th or early 17th century.

A central courtyard was created when the main house was joined to former farm buildings in the 1900s. Although the roofs have been restored in more recent times, areas of old Horsham stone slabs still survive. This sandstone material, found in Wealden clay, has a very long history and is unique to the area.

This property was once the home of Lord Baden Powell, founder of the Scout movement. Later, Sidney Poitier's agent took up residence here and held the first UK screening of In the Heat of the Night in the Great Hall in 1967.

Late Tudor

"This large farmhouse has so many different buildings – including stables, barns and even an oast– that it was difficult to find the perfect angles to draw. Eventually we chose four elevations that cover most of the estate. I love the main portrait. It shows a strong perspective along the back of the house and encompasses lots of the property's most beautiful features."

The oldest parts of this Grade II listed property were built in the fifteenth and sixteenth centuries with bay windows and close-studding. It was built in different sections with later additions in the nineteenth and twentieth centuries. The glazed windows are casement windows, three have diamond leaded panes (one with old green glass) and three have small square leaded panes.

Built by a wealthy yeoman farmer, the property remained a working farm for at least 500 years. It was once the home of actor Sir John Mills and a cottage on the estate was named Hayley Cottage after his wife Mary Hayley Bell-Mills. The property was also owned by Roger Hargreaves, creator of the Mr Men books.

Late Tudor

"This lovely thatched cottage has white walls and simple smooth corners, which give it all the fairytale features you need for a marvellous children's story. When I first saw it I felt like Red Riding Hood's grandmother was about to come out of the front door at any moment…"

The oldest parts of this Grade II listed property were built in the seventeenth century with wychert. Wychert is a clay like material used in building construction peculiar to parts of Buckinghamshire. The method of building a wychert property is similar to a cob building. To maintain the rigid nature of wychert it must not become too dry, as there is a risk of crumbling, nor too wet as there's a risk of it turning to slime.

Keeping wychert well ventilated and away from excess condensation is highly recommended. Any render applied to a wychert wall must therefore be of breathable material. So rendering wychert walls with a lime based render is common practice. The cottage's thatched roof is made of combed wheat reed hipped at both ends.

The Cottage
Eliot 2008

Late Tudor

"This fairytale house is situated in one of the nicest locations I've seen; on a hill side within a wood… it just doesn't get any better. It has breathtaking views for miles and miles. The house has lots of character and many interesting angles I could have chosen to draw. In the end we chose three elevations that, I hope, do justice to the property."

The earliest part of this Grade II listed house dates from the 16th century. Believed to have started life as two cottages, it became the Manor House and from about 1875 until after the Second World War, it housed the estate manager. It is said to have been a Royalist house during the Civil War because of its priest's hole.

The oldest section has large timber-framing and tall Tudor chimneys. Its unusual plinth contains galletted rubble. At the rear is a long cat-slide roof covering an outshot. This space once provided extra room at the back of a small house housing a service room, such as a dairy or scullery. The Victorian extension is shown clearly by a change in brick type. It has decorative white barge boarding around the roof gable.

Late Tudor

A word from the current owners:
When we first viewed the house, we were stunned to see its Tudor façade, all crooked and wonky, with smoke coming out of the chimney. It was a very warm, inviting sight. We knew immediately it was the house for us. We feel we are the custodians of the house, as if we are here to look after it and pass it on to the next owners in good order as has been done for 500 years. There is not a day that goes by where we do not appreciate the house, its history and the past. We have found several medicine bottles scattered throughout the garden (probably 19th century) and an old grenade, and there is an old red bricked well and working pump in the garden which feeds the lakes.

"This portrait is one of my favourites. The main elevation has the perfect composition… something I dream of as an artist. It sits beautifully in its surroundings and, for me, each part of the house sticks out exactly in the right place and at the right angle. It has many interesting features and elements that, together, make a great combination. I love it."

This Tudor house had a new wing added in the 1890s and a larger wing added at the turn of the century in Arts and Crafts style.
The Tudor and the mock Tudor sections of the house blend together very well. One of the previous owners was a sea captain who had a keen interest in gardening and collected seed specimens during his travels abroad.

Late Tudor

A word from the current owner:
Armed only with the estate agent's details, we drove into the
Buckinghamshire village to view Magpie Cottage. We found it
easily as it overlooks the village green. It looked, and looks, just
like a picture on a chocolate box.
We were let in by the owner and went directly into the oak
beamed dinning room, complete with its inglenook fireplace
and stone floor. The look on my wife's face told it all – this was
the place for us. Having lived here for a number of years we've
become a little blasé about the cottage; that is until we come
home from holiday, then our original joy about this charming
cottage, our home, is rekindled. My wife and I firmly believe
ourselves to be caretakers, rather than owners, of this wonderful
period property.

"Thatched roofs are a big favourite
of mine. Usually they are placed
on beamed white houses and this
combination gives lots of contrast and
brings out my pen work. This portrait
is a great example. In addition, the
strong street perspective gives the
portrait lots of depth."

This Grade II listed village property was
built in 1628. It is timber-framed with
whitewashed brick infill and blackened
rubble stone plinth. It has a thatched roof.
The interior has chamfered spine beams,
some stopped, and curved braces.
The house was a classic three bay single
dwelling which was later converted into
three cottages. It is now a single dwelling
again. The small attached barn was used by local ladies to make hats. This
picture box house was also featured in an old Hovis advertisment.

Early Georgian

Early Georgian architecture (approx 1620-1750)

The Georgian period marked the era of the Hanoverian kings, who ruled both their homeland and England when there was no clear English successor to the throne.

The reigns of George I and II are considered early Georgian. Following a period of elaborate Baroque buildings by architects such as Wren and Vanbrugh style became influenced by classical architecture. The common elements were clean lines with the emphasis on perfect symmetry, light and air.

The major influence was the work of 16th century architect Andrea Palladio whose work was seen by young English aristocrats on the Grand Tour. The features of the

Palladian style were elegance, simple decorative elements and distinct proportion and balance. Architect Inigo Jones was also an early pioneer of this movement. He was followed by Richard Boyle, the third Earl of Burlington.

Bricks were increasingly used to replace the older timber-framed style of house. Where stone was plentiful this was used, as was flint when it was available nearby.

Georgian houses had wide sash windows. These were first developed in the late 17th century with a fixed upper sash. A front door with six varying panel sizes and a pediment was the most common design for this period. The doorknocker was made from wrought iron or brass and was commonly a ring or lion's head. Doors had glass fanlights above them to illuminate the hall, which usually had a central stairway.

When the price of larger sheets of glass fell in the early 18th century six pane-over-six pane sash windows became common and four pane-over-four-pane windows were not unknown.

After 1709 London windows were required to be set back four inches from the face of the wall but the box remained exposed. Double hung sashes (both hung on cords) predominated. From about 1710 to 1730 the segmental headed arch above windows and doors was popular. The flat arch was reintroduced about the time of the accession of George II in 1727.

Country estates

Large country house estates were given landscaped gardens with classical temples, grottoes and bridges. Sometimes complete villages were cleared to create better views from the country house.

Eating, drinking, playing cards and dancing became a serious business for the very wealthy classes and so houses were designed for these activities. Elegant rooms displayed cornices, door arches, shutters, dados and window seats.

For the growing middle classes imitation was on a lesser scale and the standard house layout was two storeys high and two rooms deep throughout, plus an attic for servants' accommodation and a basement. The front door was centrally placed between regularly spaced multi-paned sash windows. Cornices were commonly embellished with decorative mouldings and painted white.

Terraces

Most typical of the Georgian period were the terraces of houses that were built in towns. Significant urban expansion led to a need for houses to be spaced more closely. This need was met by joining tall, narrow dwellings together in a stylish row, often shaped in a semi circle like the famous circus in Bath.

Floorboards were limed and waxed and ceilings were lime plastered. Internal doors often had windows above them, which allowed more light into the large, square, high ceilinged rooms. Areas prone to become grubby through frequent use, such as doors and skirting boards, were painted dark brown. Windows were enclosed by wooden shutters which folded back during the day. At night these were concealed with decorative curtains.

In the 17th and most of the 18th century lighting came almost entirely from fires or candles. Candles were used sparingly even in homes of the wealthy. They were positioned where light was needed or carried from room to room.

Some fixed lights were used in larger houses in the form of sconces, hall lights and chandeliers in the most important rooms, although these were only lit on special occasions.

Fire surrounds were frequently made of marble and hob grates first appeared around 1720. A central duck's nest held the fire where the ash easily filtered through, with hobs on either side to keep kettles and pots warm. This time was a period of tremendous change for fireplaces, with each succeeding design seeking to improve heat radiation without smoke entering the room.

During the Georgian period thought was first given to home sanitary conditions and various devices were introduced to improve the basic arrangements already in use; often simply a small building in the garden. However, even when a recognisable water closet was invented, the drainage system left much to be desired until the early 19th century.

J.D.

Early Georgian

"Living in a row of cottages or an end-of-terrace house can be a wonderful journey into ancient times, with lots of history and character, particularly if it's a beautiful and lovely house like this one and situated in a beautiful little village. I believe lots of detached house owners would be keen to swap their homes with one of these cottages…"

This 18th century Grade II listed cottage is set in a picturesque Kent village and is one of a row of cottages that was formerly a public house. The tile hanging on the upper storey protects the timber frame underneath. This is a common device used in this part of the country and makes use of good local clays. Tile hanging appears in several designs. The style on this house is called Fish Scale. Thinner than roof tiles, these tiles are hung on wooden pegs – oak, hazel or willow – which are in turn fixed to the timber frame.

The lower brick storey has been painted and modern framing applied. The flat hood with brackets above the front door was a feature introduced in the late 17th century, continuing until about 1750.

Eli Ofir 2010

Early Georgian

"The L-shape structure of this old house blends beautifully in with the surrounding area. The flint stone also blends beautifully with the brickwork around the windows, and the garden gives the house more atmosphere and character all around. The dogs, of course add their own glamour to the portrait."

This picturesque house lies in a small rural village in Kent. The oldest part of the house is thought to date as far back as the 17th century. Many changes have been made since then, including incarnations as a village Post Office, shop and Telephone Exchange. It is now home to a former Conservative MP. Using locally sourced flints for several

of the exterior walls, the building structure also features warm red bricks on others. Bricks quoins on the house corners and jambs of the same material around the windows bring some uniformity to the haphazard arrangement of the uncut flints.

Early Georgian

A *word from the current owners:*

It's believed 'John Gylbert gentleman built a capital messuage' on the present site of The Red House in 1631. The present house was probably built for Charles Couchman. In 1688 Dr Thomas Fuller, a famous pharmacist, became the owner. He wrote a book of prescriptions and left on record his views about the excellence of beer and the risks of tobacco smoking.

Francis Austen purchased the house in 1743 and the building remained in the ownership of the Austen family until 1913. Since March 1936 our firm has occupied The Red House. It's on the south side of town and one of the most distinguished buildings in Sevenoaks. We greatly value its historical connections and are proud to be based in such a handsome building.

    Knocker & Foskett Solicitors

"*Every time I used to drive along Sevenoaks high street I nearly crashed into the car in front as I was always so distracted by this magnificent classic Georgian building. I needed to draw it! Thank God I got the commission from the law firm that occupies it. I love the building and the portrait and I am at rest with my obsession now. Drive safely.*"

This imposing red brick Grade II* listed building dates from 1686. It has the typical characteristics of a William and Mary house, such as a moulded stone band above its ground floor windows, a deeply carved cornice and Doric columns on either side of the front door.

While it's now a solicitors' office, it was previously a private house owned by Dr Francis Austen, the great uncle of Jane Austen. The famous author stayed here in the summer of 1788.

The Red House
Fl Ofic 2004

Early Georgian

A word from the current owner:
It was love at first sight when we saw the house. We'd seen over 50 houses and nothing created a 'Wow!' moment like this one. Despite being a large house the rooms aren't massive, so there's a feeling of warmth and cosiness even on the coldest, darkest winter days.
We have made some improvements to the house and gone into areas which weren't originally intended for human habitation – it's been very interesting to see what was once the hayloft seamlessly changed into a gym. It now looks totally in keeping.

"To get a whole view of the back of the house (the original front of the house) I had to tie some trees out of the way and so change the composition. This made the main features visible, especially the magnificent round two tower-like ends of the back wall. Together with the huge door and entrance pillars it looks like a house built for royalty…"

This Grade II listed property was burnt down in 1716 and rebuilt in 1722. The central porch has fluted Doric columns, a triglyph frieze and a semi-circular fanlight. There are later additions from the Victorian period. The first documents relating to it are from 1646 when it was a farm. In the 1880s the house was occupied by a wealthy retired brewer who had four live-in servants.

Early Georgian

"This house is so huge it took me ages to figure out how to get all of its front elevation into one portrait while still recording all the beauty of the detail and achieving good perspective and depth. The result is that my portrait really shows the whole house, but I also wanted to zoom in and draw only the middle section of the building. So I added a close up version of the front, the fifth portrait I drew of this estate. The back view, with its round porch and the stables, was also magnificent to draw."

This fine Grade I country house in East Kent was built for a high ranking aristocratic family by Robert Adam in the mid Georgian period of the 1760s. It was one of his early works after returning from Rome and coming under the influence of the new Palladian movement. The result can be seen here in a regular rectangular central block with straight balustraded corridors leading to similarly shaped wings on either side. The corridor sections features several niches containing statues. The central section of the main block projects to accentuate the banded plinth with its simple frieze and cornice parapet, with triangular pediment.

A flight of nine moulded steps leads up to the front panelled door with a semi-circular fanlight below a pediment, which is also triangular and supported on columns. All the symmetrically spaced windows have stone moulded surrounds. The building is predominantly constructed of red bricks (about three million of them) with Portland stone dressing and a slate roof. It originally cost just £20,000. Following the Second World War the property became a school. It stayed that way until fairly recently, but has now returned to residential accommodation with a restaurant adjacent to the walled garden.

Early Georgian

"This wonderful building is inspiring and stands out from the surrounding landscape. I love the huge chimney in the back view portrait. It has a distinguished and glamorous look to it. The property and grounds must be a wonderful campus for students."

Hall Place in Burchetts Green is the home of Berkshire College of Agriculture. It is appropriately situated in 400 acres of landscaped grounds, which once included a deer park. This setting enhances the Grade I listed building dating from 1728. It was constructed when the old manor house was demolished by William East and replaced by this classic early Georgian design that took seven years to complete.

A flight of stone steps with an ornamental balustrade leads up to impressive double doors in a door-case with panelled pilasters, leaf and scroll capitals with moulded cornice and pediment. This is the most extravagant decoration on the front façade, as the red brick is the background to twenty-six windows arranged over four storeys of the square central section. Two wings join this part via one storey blocks, which have a plain stone frieze below a panelled brick parapet echoing the more extravagant version on the main building. The East family kept possession of this property until the early 1800s, when it passed to a nephew, George Clayton, who added East to his name. The last Clayton East to reside at The Hall was Robert, a young adventurer whose life formed the basis of the film The English Patient.

Early Georgian

"This is a dream house for artists. The contrast of the white and stone walls, the unique and beautiful chimneys, the huge windows and the roof…this house was a delight to draw. It has a magical feel to it and I wanted just to keep on looking at it. It's one of my favourites.."

This grand stone house started life as a lodge for the estate of a nearby mansion. In the mid-1800s it was considerably enlarged and became the home of two successive solicitors. By 1881, after more improvements, a retired Colonel of the Indian Army moved in. He was a survivor and hero of the Punjab and Indian Mutiny campaigns. Following a late marriage he raised a family here. He and his wife employed four live in servants and also a nursemaid to care for their two young daughters. A coachman and his family lived in a cottage in the grounds. The Colonel died in 1927, followed eventually by his much younger wife in 1944. However, the house was sold in 1937 and sales particulars quoted eight bedrooms, four reception rooms, a stable cottage, two tennis courts, and fruit and kitchen gardens in six acres of land – all for £2,250

Late Georgian

Late Georgian architecture (approx 1750-1810)

Late Georgian architecture spanned the reigns of George III and the Prince Regent, who became George IV. During this time style became more elaborate, with the archaeological discoveries of Greece and Italy inspiring architects to embark upon a Neo-classicist revival.

Robert Adam and Sir John Soane were two of the most prominent exponents of this revival. Although Adam implemented brightly coloured interiors with Byzantine and Etruscan motifs, this was balanced by understated ornamentation. He developed the concept of one scheme for all the elements of the room such as walls, ceiling and furniture.

It was during the mid-Georgian period that Robert Adam and his brother James published the first of three volumes of Works in Architecture. This publication standardised a range of details and ornamental design that could be used for entrances, fireplaces, ceilings and wall friezes. This resulted in the first mass production of stick-on mouldings by numerous manufacturers.

Standardisation

Much of the standardisation of Georgian house design can be traced back to the introduction of building legislation after the Great Fire of London in 1666. Over a period of years restrictions were gradually imposed on such things as the height of rooms, structural thickness of party and external walls and the size of timbers for floors and roofs. It was as a result of new fire regulations that roofs were hidden by a parapet wall.

After 1774 windows were required to be recessed behind an outer nib of masonry to prevent the spread of fire from one to another. This development, together with the introduction of finer glazing bars, led to the emergence of the style of window so characteristic of the mid-Georgian period.

Excise duty on glass generally favoured the use of small light panes of crown glass. The introduction of small margin lights around a large central pane, fashionable in the 1820s, was an elegant but significantly more expensive departure from the usual six-over-six panes sash window.

The window tax was not repealed until 1851 and therefore, to avoid excessive payments, a number of house owners bricked up their windows. However, blocked windows were also used to achieve symmetry and are common in Georgian houses.

Late Georgian houses might have some Rococo embellishments of flowing decoration while still keeping their symmetrical exterior. Some architects led a Gothic revival, but more successful was the Chinoiserie trend of the Regency period (approximately from 1811-1830). This was used extensively for the interior of the Royal Pavilion in Brighton while the exterior presents a flamboyant Indian influenced style.

Sanitation

In the mid-eighteenth century sanitary conditions were appalling with virtually no sewers. Household waste, including that from the privy, fed into open ditches and then into cesspools and on into the nearest river or sea. Only the larger town houses had a privy or closet erected over a cesspit in the back yard or garden. Most households used chamber pots or commodes especially at night.

Many dining rooms of wealthy families had chamber pots hidden behind curtains or in a cupboard to be mostly used by men. The first water closets were invented around 1775 but the overall situation did not improve until the development of public drainage systems in the late 19th century.

Another major innovation was the increased incorporation of gardens within overall house layouts. The Georgian garden heralded the start of the modern English passion for gardening.

D.J.

Late Georgian

A word from the current owner:

We're very lucky to have found such a wonderful place to live and to be successful in business at the same time. For more than five years I've worked almost every day in the pub. Above the bars, the front room of our home looks out over the marketplace; I wonder what sights people would have seen looking out over the same view a hundred or more years ago?

The pub hasn't changed much in the way it looks. It just keeps going, marching on through wars, depression and times of celebration and joy. We have a ghost or spirit presence here. Sometimes before we open I'll be at the bar getting things prepared and feel the sensation of someone or something just brushing past me or pulling my shirt sleeve – very gentle, as if it's a girl or frail woman.

"I visit Henley-on-Thames frequently for my work. The beautiful town centre always intrigues me. For years I wanted to draw the Argyll. It is one of the town's most famous pubs and an icon for visitors. I was fortunate enough to get a commission and, since then, every time I visit to eat the pub's lovely food I sit under my portrait hanging on the wall."

The Argyll Public House has had a number of interesting names during its brewing history. In the 1840s it was known as the North Star, then the Cannon Inn.

In 1872, it briefly became the Hop Leaf, a very fitting name for the establishment and the trade mark of the Simonds Brewery. Finally, in the late 1880s, it became The Argyll. The building was rebuilt with brick in the mid-Victorian period, with three floors and a carriage entrance on its east side. The mock Tudor front was added in 1919.

Late Georgian

"This is the home of my Osteopath, so it's a personal thing for me. He saved me from a chronic back problem. I visited him for nearly eight months on a weekly basis and loved his old house more and more. When I was back on my feet again I wanted to thank him in an original way, so I drew his house as a gift. It holds a very warm place in my heart. Thank you so much Trevor."

This country style two storey brick house was built in the late Georgian period. It has sliding sash windows. The open porch is typical of this period and the roof is made up of grey slate tiling. A small former milking parlour has been converted into a snug reading room. During the Victorian period the house was occupied by a number of farmers. In the 1850s, it was occupied by Edward and Elizabeth Penfold and their thirteen children.

Early Victorian

Early Victorian architecture (approx 1837-1860)

The Victorian style is the name given to the architecture of the reign of Queen Victoria (1837-1901). Victorian buildings still dominate our towns and cities. Stylistically and technically, early Victorian architecture is a world away from late Victorian architecture. The early Victorian style was labelled classical or Gothic. The classical style derived from the architecture of ancient Greece and Rome, the Gothic is more exotic and influenced by Chinese, Egyptian and Moorish architecture. The 1850s and 1860s saw a Queen Anne revival.

Industrial revolution

The Industrial Revolution brought innovative techniques and opened up worldwide trade, and the ensuing rapid economic growth led to a big increase in building.

With the creation of the railways and many new manufacturing processes, locally produced building materials, previously only used in their immediate areas, soon became available all over the country.

The expanding empire also provided cheap imports and a variety of styles and ideas. The population grew rapidly and towns and cities expanded into the surrounding countryside. A defined middle class emerged, with new spending power, who wanted to copy the aristocracy. Land acquired a new value for building and the large scale developer made his appearance.

With towns fast expanding, and poor quality houses erected for the workers (crammed ill lit, insanitary dwellings), diseases such as cholera and typhoid became rife. These diseases had no respect for social status; Prince Albert died of typhoid in 1861.
In the 1850s, the stench of the Thames, by now an open sewer, forced the Houses of Parliament to introduce a series of public health and building Acts which laid down the requirements for drainage, waste disposal, refuse collection and water supply. The Victorian legislators strengthened the powers and responsibilities of the local authorities.

Suburban villa

The early Victorian period also saw the arrival of the Suburban villa, built for the growing numbers of industrialists, merchants and professional men, to reflect their social status and wealth.

The term villa is taken from the finely proportioned renaissance style houses built in the 18th century. These new properties were usually built in the suburbs, close to factories, mills or offices. They were built mainly of brick, which offered the greatest variety both in methods of bonding and type.

Regionally coloured bricks became available. London brick, for example, is yellowy, Cambridge brick is white, and Kent and Sussex bricks are both splendid shades of red. Some villas were built of good quality brick, but poor quality brickwork was often covered over with elaborate decoration. Stone was used if it was available locally.

The owners of Suburban Villas wanted their properties to reflect private ownership, with gates and railings offering both protection and a display of wealth. The strip of land from the gate to the entrance door provided another change, proclaiming the status of the owner. Paths were made of tiles, stone flags or gravel. First impressions were important to the Victorians and the grand front doors reflected this.

Windows

The range and variety of windows also increased dramatically during the 19th century. They were derived from two main types – sash and casement. New glassmaking technology and the abolition of the window tax in 1851 made larger panes of glass available and transformed the look of Victorian windows. The size and shape of windows came to reflect the importance of house owners.

By the mid 19th century there was a heaviness and solidity in the architecture, more influenced by the Italian style than the classical. Windows had elaborate moulded architraves and doors became more intricate.

In the 1830's the Victorian upper classes were not only very rich, but were getting richer mainly by investing in the Industrial Revolution. They were also in virtual control of the government, the armed forces and the church. This enabled the remodelling of their country houses or a complete new build.

Country estates

The prosperity of Victorian agriculture also gave the landowning classes' greater wealth which they invested into country estates. Between 1835 and 1889 a total of 500 country houses were built or remodelled. Each of these houses had estates of at least several hundred acres. Enormous fortunes were made by the aspiring and socially ambitious middle classes and country estates were in great demand.

The Victorian gentleman's house was substantial, dignified and suitable for the rank of the owner. The architecture was a mixture of piety, snobbery, romanticism, idealism and pretentiousness. The size of the house was dictated by the number of people it had to contain.

Many large country houses had forty or more indoor and outdoor staff. The household was divided into family, guests and staff, each with its own wing or portion. One curious feature of the Victorian house was the addition of the sacrosanct male domain. The nucleus of this male preserve was the billiard room.

R.C.

Early Victorian

A word from the current owner:
We fell in love with Wilsley Oast the moment we saw it and we have been its proud owners for the past fourteen years. It has character and its history reflects its original purpose as a working building, drying hops for the brewing industry.. The opportunity to enjoy it stems principally from hops now being sourced from overseas, making our oast houses redundant. The conversion of Wilsley Oast to residential use has enabled us to fulfill our dream.

Wilsley has two roundels with conical roofs capped by distinctive rotational cowls, designed to enable the fires used for drying hops to escape through the roof without letting rain in. The two roundels enclose four round rooms. These take some getting used to as there are no corners as there are in a conventional square room. There is also an echo effect when you stand and speak in the centre of the room.

"What a classic Kent Oast House this is! The two oasts sit beautify together and blend into the house itself. Both the front and the back view are perfectly balanced, giving me a great composition to draw. I loved the little round window in the joining up wall between the oasts, with its own sliding curved roof... perfect."

Despite hops being introduced to Kent as early as the 16th century, the familiar roundel shape of the Kent countryside home was an invention of John Read of Horsmonden in the 1790s. The name oast house comes from the Latin aidis (hearth or house) and aestus meaning heat. This Kent oast house, once attached to the local farm, is believed to have been built in the mid 1800s. It was converted into a residential building in about 1960. The year 1878 was the peak of hop farming in Britain, when Kent contributed just under two thirds of the total acreage.

In the first week of September Kent was invaded by itinerant gipsy hop pickers and London East Enders, who picked the golden yellow resin glands required in brewing. The hops were trained up poles or strings to a height of 16-20 feet. They were eventually cut down by stilt walkers, before their flowers were torn from the foliage.

Early Victorian

"I love the white raised corner quoins on this lovely Kent town house. Although they are white on a light painted front wall the contrast is strong, giving it the classic Victorian touch. The back view is so different from the front. It's as if it is not the same house at all."

The lines of this mid-Victorian town house in Kent are simple with classical details. The white raised corner quoins contrast with the stuccoed brick walls to accentuate the clean lines of the building. The plain walls are a reminder of the white stone houses previously built by Decimus Burton in nearby Tunbridge Wells.

The decorative brackets above the second floor windows add to the raised stone effect surrounding all of the twelve-pane sash windows and the lines of white cornices at first and second floor level. The rear elevation, however, is simple brickwork. The semi-detached arrangement, a new innovation of the time, allowed for more living space within suburban developments. The house has always been residential although, at one time, it was divided into flats. However, in the early days one of the occupants was a famous clock and watchmaker called Frederick Joseph Barraud. He was also the founder of the Guildhall Clockmaker's Museum in London. He stayed in the house with his daughter until his death in 1859.

Early Victorian

"Cotswold limestone is always lovely to draw, especially in this instance as I was given the wonderful opportunity to recreate how the barn would have looked as a working barn. I worked with a house historian who provided old archive plans and maps of the property and, using additional information on the use of the barn, we came up with this artist's impression of the past. I love it. I also drew some elevations of the current house and it's wonderful to compare the old with the renovated."

This large Grade II listed barn was built in the mid-nineteenth century with dressed limestone which was quarried locally. A smaller barn to the east of the property was built in the eighteenth century.

The main barn was built as a threshing barn, to loosen the grains of corn and separate them from the stalks. The tall doors provided light and access for carts to collect the corn. The storage bays were either side of the main threshing floor.

In the winter the barn gave shelter to farm animals. Threshing was mechanised by the 1920s and the barn became a milking parlour. It was converted to residential use in the mid-1990s, but earlier agricultural workers would have also used it for accommodation.

Early Victorian

"I love the square porch of this house. It looks so clean and yet stands tall like a bell tower. The porch arch, together with the arched windows, makes the house appear very fresh and soft, especially as it stands in the middle of the countryside at the bottom of a hill. What a magnificent contrast."

This house has had a varied history since its construction in the mid 1800s. Starting life as a substantial Victorian villa, one of its residents was Henry Holiday, a stained glass artist and Pre-Raphaelite painter. In the Second World War it was used by a major building society to store important records during the London Blitz. After the War it became a children's home, but in recent times it has been restored to its original purpose as a residential property.

The effect of the stuccoed brick walls emphasises the clean, symmetrical design of the house. The four pane central windows are typical of this time, just before larger sheets of glass became more readily available. The arched shape over the windows has an Italian influence as has the square porch, reminiscent of a bell tower. The slate hipped roof has a shallow pitch. Further ornamentation is shown in decorated stone brackets and a raised brick string at first floor level. The imposing entrance at first floor level via stone steps suggests that the ground floor was once the service area.

Early Victorian

A word from the current owner:
We've lived in Court Lodge since it was first converted - you can still see the outline of the furnace beneath our dining room floor. We were drawn to both the house and the surrounding countryside. We thought it'd make a lovely family home, which it has done. We've brought up our two daughters here. It's a spacious house and the thickness of its solid walls keeps it cool in summer and warm in winter.

"This corner oast house is part of an eight (eight!!) oast structure. It's so wonderful to look at all the eight Cowls and see how all the wind vane's turn in the same direction, each featuring a different little black figure – some horses, bears and pigs. The oast houses you mainly see in Kent are round. but this one stands out for its straight rectangular lines."

This classic Grade II listed Kentish double roundel oast house, was part of a planned farmyard attached to a working farm. Built of ragstone in about 1840, it was converted to a habitable dwelling in 1983.

An oast house is used to dry fresh hops before they are sent to the brewers for flavouring beer. A traditional oast house consists of two sections - the oast, which

was a kiln, and the stowage, which was the barn with a cooling floor and press at first floor and storage area at ground level. A planned or model farmyard was an 18th-19th century experimental farm, used to research and demonstrate improvements in agricultural techniques, efficiency and building layout. It was usually designed around a courtyard plan. Farm buildings were designed, sometimes by notable architects, to be beautiful as well as utilitarian.

Eli Ofir 2008

Early Victorian

"It wasn't easy at all to get such a large structure onto one page or to convey the feel of the whole building and include its details. After a long struggle I managed to catch the right angle and composition. I wanted to draw an additional zoom in portrait from the same angle, to give more detail and do justice to all the elements that are too small for the large view. It's a beautiful example of a Victorian town house."

This mid-Victorian end of terrace house was built in 1871. It was built with large sash windows and an impressive stepped entrance. The row of six houses was built by a Miss Portal as an orphanage and named the Home for Friendless Boys. The home catered for up to 200 boys aged 10 to 16 who "have lost their character or are in danger of losing it". The boys learnt carpentry, shoemaking, gardening and how to look after horses. The exterior was built to resemble a terrace of normal houses, but the interior was one whole building. The orphanage closed in 1903 and, after a variety of uses, was converted into six buildings in the 1990s.

Late Victorian

Late Victorian architecture (approx 1860-1901)

As the great Victorian building boom continued, its visual results became increasingly dominant. More and more fields and orchards were swallowed up by new housing estates, and more and more factories and slums were created around larger and larger industrial towns.

The late Victorian period brought legislation giving local authorities the power to compel owners to make good unsound and insanitary properties. Private builders now had strict building controls.

A growing middle class of office workers, managers, shopkeepers and craftsmen who were respectable, hardworking and ambitious, spurred the development of the suburbs, making it possible to escape the town and city centres via the new railway and tram systems. These new houses were often built in superior terraces with a garden in the rear. They often had Welsh slate roofs and embellishments in various styles.

House designs could be chosen from a basic pattern book with the homeowner incorporating their ideas and personal preferences. Features included towers, bay windows, balconies, and a partial or full porch sweeping around the first floor. Stained glass windows were also very popular.

The houses had good size rooms with plenty of intricate detailing in their reception rooms and bedrooms. Running water, gas lighting and other amenities were also present. Interiors were opulent, featuring heavy curtains and wallpapers in rich, dark colours. Rooms were often overfilled with furniture and objects. If you were well-to-do you even had an indoor toilet. Otherwise it was a shed in the backyard.
The middle class late Victorian home was also a place where the family could communicate their social status through their domestic arrangements and their distance from the working class, including their servants. This had a high impact on the design of the middle class Victorian houses, as there had to be separate entrances for staff and even different stairwells so servants were placed away from the family. Cheaper glass gave ordinary Victorians the opportunity to build conservatories, adding glamour to their homes. Glasshouse and conservatory builders offered prefabricated products through catalogues. The grander Victorian mansions were built with lodges at gated entrances and had leisure gardens with extensive greenhouses and stable blocks.

Agricultural slump

The 1870's – with industry and agriculture booming and British prestige at its height – became the golden age of Victorian country house building as it was of most other aspects of Victorian life.

This was brought to an abrupt end with the agricultural slump of 1879-1894, mainly due to disastrous harvests and the influx of cheap American corn. By the late Victorian period the social prestige of a country home remained the same, but increasing numbers contented themselves with a main house in London and a weekend or holiday home in the country. The seaside villa became increasing popular.
The Arts and Crafts design of architecture flourished from 1880-1910. The Arts and Crafts movement was instigated by the designer, artist, poet, writer and socialist William Morris, and inspired by the writer John Ruskin, who thought the machine

was at the root of many social ills and that a healthy society depended on skilled and creative workers.

The Movement advocated truth to materials and traditional craftsmanship. It was a reaction to the styles that had developed out of machine production. The use of traditional skills and creativity revived old techniques and many of their styles were sixteenth and seventeenth century in origin.

The Arts and Crafts style was simple in form and drew on the vernacular traditions of the British countryside. One of the best known architects during this period was Sir Edwin Lutyens who created Old English style houses.

By the end of the nineteenth century, the Arts and Crafts Movement had influenced architecture, painting, graphics, stained glass, metalwork, wallpaper, textiles, furniture and woodwork.

R.C.

Late Victorian

A word from the current owner:

The imposing front door takes your breath away… On our first viewing I said to my wife I want that front door. We were only able to buy one half of the house at a time as it was divided and the half that was available at first did not include the front door I'd set my heart on. Eventually we had the opportunity to purchase the second half of the house. It was then the real fun began.

As a family we travel extensively. Whenever we return home the understated grandeur, the solidity of the design, emanates security and welcoming like no other house. It's so reassuring to step through the front door and be enveloped by the house. The house comes alive when it is full of family, in particular our young lively grandchildren. It resonates with squeals of delight as they roar round exploring and enjoying every nook and cranny.

"This is a breathtaking house comprising of all the characteristics that make a property perfect to draw (and probably to live in). It is constructed of so many building materials…brick, wood, stone, tiles… it's just a magnificent structure."

This substantial late Victorian house Grade II* listed house has many characteristics of the English Revival style. Mock timber-framing, mullioned windows and prominent chimneys all feature. The protruding front gables were a popular design of the influential architect Richard Norman Shaw. Born in Edinburgh in 1831, he developed his own style based on English vernacular buildings, which he was to use on numerous town and country houses until 1895.

Shaw was commissioned by John Lane Shrub, a young local landowner who was living here in 1871 with his young family. Also in residence were a parlour maid, a cook, a nurse, a housemaid and a coachman..

During the Second World War the house was used to house evacuee children. After this it was divided into three dwellings. It is now restored to its original state as one house.

Late Victorian

"What intrigued me most in this house was the very strong contrast of old and new. The modern glass additions seamlessly grow out through the old parts of the house. The transparent roof and black steel poles (which light up the entire interior and bring so much light into the house) appear to naturally spring from the beautiful old Victorian Coach House. It's a simply amazing structure."

This house was formally the stables and coach house of a large country estate built in the 1870s. In 1889 the estate was purchased by Sir Frank Crisp, an eccentric Victorian solicitor responsible for drafting the first London Stock Exchange Rules and involved in the financing of the London Underground system. It was later purchased by George Harrison of The Beatles. The house was converted from stables in the 1970s and many of the original architectural features remain, including the candy twist brick and stone chimney and Latin inscribed columns. A saddling up glass atrium was constructed over part of the courtyard in the 1920s.

Late Victorian

"Getting to see the whole of the front of this house through the many surrounding trees was a challenge. When I stitched a number of photos together the whole beauty of the house was revealed in its spectacular Victorian layout."

This grand Victorian, Queen Ann style, house was built in 1883. It was designed by the architect William Henry Crossland. He also built Royal Holloway University which was opened in 1886 by Queen Victoria.

The house is reputed to have been built as a home for the Crossland family until the building of the university was completed. A number of houses were built along the drive, back to front, with their doors facing away from the road. Their front doors are accessed from the rear garden.

Late Victorian

A *word from the current owner:*
'Wow!' was the one word that summed up our initial impression when we drove through the gates of the property for the first time. We were amazed to think we could possibly live in such a stunning house and we were overwhelmed by its many beautiful period features – and that's just on the outside. Our initial appreciation of its architecture is still with us, particularly when we return after spending time away.

During renovations we climbed the scaffolding to roof level and viewed a weather vane on one of the parapets. It was marked with the initials CLH and the date 1896. CLH stands for Charles Lang Huggins, one of the early owners of the house. It is thought that he added a number of extensions to the property to accommodate his growing family – he and his wife had a total of nine children. The house they inhabited was much larger than the one we live in today. Rumour has it that the servants had to walk about a quarter of a mile from the kitchen to serve food in the dining room.

"W*hen I first set my eyes on this house I was lost for words. A faint voice came out of my throat…it sounded something like 'wooo'! The house is so different from anything I'd seen before. It's just spectacular. After I worked my way around it, drawing each corner, window and tower, I became even more astonished by its wonderful design. It's a real work of art and I hope my drawing of it did it at least some justice."*

This grand Victorian mansion was built around 1896. Its design is typical of the Arts and Crafts Movement with turrets and balconies. Its first known owner was Benjamin Hall, who also played an important role in building the village church and the school. He was succeeded by his great nephew Charles Lang Huggins, a stockbroker.

The house would once have been the focal point of the village and many of the surrounding houses were owned by the family, along with some 200 acres of the surrounding countryside. The house that Charles Huggins took over from his uncle bore little resemblance to the property he left on his death. The immensity of the property he created is said to have been the result of him having a very large family of nine children. It's rumoured that once Charles had completed his extensions to the property there was a distance of 100 yards from the kitchen to the dining room. The house totalled 30 bedrooms and had an equal number of staff. A large portion of the house was later demolished.

Late Victorian

"This beautiful townhouse has a very strong presence. It sits on a street corner overlooking other houses and gives me the feeling of a solid and well grounded structure. The combination of Mock Tudor beams with brickwork and stone window frames has a very powerful feel to it."

Situated in one of the famous residential parks of Royal Tunbridge Wells, this late Victorian house was erected in 1898 by Louis Beale and Son, a Tunbridge developer and builder.

He used Tudor style timber-framing and added a decorative white painted balcony, features that remained popular for many years after. The first occupant, auctioneer Henry Wickenden, lived here for at least 24 years with his household of seven children, a cook and housemaid.

Late Victorian

"It took me hours just to get the composition for this portrait right. The house is so complex and detailed, with lots of features and corners. The front view took about four and a half photos from a distance to capture, and I needed to stitch them together before I was able to grasp the whole layout."

This house is thought to have been built at the end of the 1800s. It was initially a dower house to a much larger property owned by a wealthy Irish wine and spirit merchant and his large household. After the larger house burned down in the early 1900s this surviving property experienced many changes, including a succession of different names. For a while it was a temporary hospital for the war wounded. It also took delivery of precious items from London museums and galleries for safe keeping during the War.

The building is now divided into several flats. It retains, though, much of its late Victorian architecture, influenced in this instance by the Tudor era. Several of these details continued to be used into the Edwardian age include painted timber-framing, decorative tile hanging and chimneystacks with multiple flues.

Edwardian

Edwardian architecture (approx 1901-1920)

Although surrounded by a wealth of technological advances such as electricity, cars, aeroplanes, wireless and telephones, the Edwardians rejected modernity.

This had a marked effect on interior design and architecture. The fashion was for handmade crafts, rustic cottages and country ways, which produced an eclectic mix of styles used by builders to appeal in a fashion conscious age.

The rise in house building continued to sweep away many poorer slums, replacing them with terraced housing. Better quality developments set in wide tree-lined roads also appeared. The most striking feature of these larger houses was their construction. Generally the materials were of a high quality. The most popular structures were built in red brick, usually manufactured in local brickworks.

Improvements in drainage systems, together with larger plots, helped make the private rear garden an important feature and were frequently included in architects' plans. This changed the appearance and plan of the rear of Edwardian houses.

Rather than being faced in cheap bricks as before and only viewed by servants, the new back garden was now another part of the house – so the rear façade had as much attention paid to it as the front. Balconies were also popular and sometimes had French windows, typically painted white and often purely decorative.

The Arts and Crafts style of house featured clay tile cladding on the upper storey of the front elevation. The upper storey at the rear gables had mock timber-framing and pebbledash. Although this artistic movement advocated better quality, handmade materials usually proved too expensive for most general housing and therefore builders incorporated only elements of the fashion.

Edwardian

Classical design

Unlike Victorian architects, architects of the Edwardian era also created houses based on classical design. Queen Anne style houses featured prominent chimneys, Dutch and Flemish gables, tall, square and angled bay windows and white painted window frames and stonework.

The other classically inspired fashion was neo-Georgian. This was a reflection of the late 17th and early 18th century style based on simple, elegant lines and featuring plain brick, symmetrical front elevations (sometimes softened with decorative string courses) and white cornices underneath the eaves. Semi-circular fanlights were inserted above front doors. Flush fitted sash windows and shallow arches on dormers were also incorporated.

The plans of large detached houses changed in several ways from their predecessors. Servants' conditions improved as they became harder to find and retain. Previously service rooms had usually been confined to basements, but now they became incorporated into the body of the house at the side or rear of living rooms. The change to a less ornate design in door furniture and skirting boards showed the division between servant and master.

Windows

The three main styles of windows in the Edwardian period were sash, mullioned and casement. Roofs were either covered in slate, which could now be transported cheaply from Wales, or by clay tiles requiring a steeper elevation because of the extra weight.

Halls also underwent dramatic changes. In Victorian times they'd shrunk to a narrow passage but now they were revived as meeting places. In some houses the front door opened into a multi-purpose room, while in others the hall was a grand central space with the main staircase leading off it.

Black and white geometric floor tiles were typical of this age when thought had to be given to the practicality of cleaning, especially when servants were in short supply.

Art Nouveau was another favoured design element inspired by the simple forms of Japanese art of undulating lines and themes from the natural world. It was often featured on stained glass windows, tiling in bathrooms and fireplaces.

Fireplaces

Fireplaces and their surrounds were possibly the most important feature of rooms, not just as a source of heat but also as a focal point. Following technological advances of the Victorian period, grates were becoming increasingly efficient at reflecting maximum heat with minimum smoke.

The influence of the Arts and Crafts movement produced a variety of designs such as polished metal smoke hoods or wooden mantles, which provided extra shelving for display. Brick and tile fireplaces were a modern classic design of the time, with craft tiles – floral, animal or medieval or exotic – on the splayed sides of the grate. Another popular pattern was blue and white Delft.

Bathrooms were also standard in most houses by this time, although they were often small as people still washed in the bedroom at a washstand with a basin and jug of hot water brought by a servant. By the 1890s most middle class houses had a separate WC in a small room upstairs rather than outside adjoining the house.

Electricity

In this transitional stage gas mantles were first installed as a method of lighting. They gradually replaced oil lamps and candles.

The initial spread of electricity was slow among ordinary people as it was so much more expensive than gas. It was not until around 1911 when metal filament lamps were perfected, that electric lighting became more widely available.

Even by the First World War electric lighting was still enjoyed solely by the rich minority. It was only after the Electricity (Supply) Act of 1926 was passed that real progress was made in distribution.

Kitchens

A cooking range dominated the Edwardian kitchen; a cast iron combination of oven, hotplates and boiler heated by a central fire. Built-in cupboards were becoming standard, although freestanding dressers with open shelves were sometimes fitted.

Often a shallow sink, usually with just one tap supplying cold water, was situated in an adjoining scullery. This was used for washing clothes and would also contain a copper for heating water, a mangle, and a wooden clothes airer suspended from the ceiling.

The development of ready mixed and prepared foods such as butter reduced the need for other specialist rooms. A walk-in larder contained dairy products and other perishable food. It was kept as cool as possible by incorporating a gauze-covered open window and tiled floor. The servants' hall was usually conveniently placed next to the service rooms and had its own fireplace.

Bedrooms were generally lighter and less ornate than rooms on the ground floor. Most had fireplaces but in the main fires were only lit if somebody was ill. Nurseries were given more consideration at this time, providing single sex bedrooms and a room for play and education, positioned to catch as much sun as possible.

J.D.

Edwardian

"What fascinating features are those white symbols hanging over the main windows of the ground floor and the sundial above the main entrance! This house stands out from the other houses on its street, it seems to hold lots of secrets within its walls…"

This Edwardian house was built in 1904 by the Architects Edwin Otto Sachs and George Spencer Hoffman. It was built on the site of five late Victorian houses that were demolished. It has a number of unique features that indicate that it was designed for personal use.

The house was built as the family home for George Hoffman who lived here with his wife Charlotte and their son Henry and three live in staff. Sachs and Hoffman Architects had offices in Pall Mall, London and their work is connected to a number British Theatres.

Edwardian

"When I was drawing this house I imagined Juliet standing on the balcony waiting for Romeo. The balcony just looks so romantic and gives a soft, smooth and feminine feel to the brick built house."

Dating from 1906, this house is typical of the late Victorian and early Edwardian age. The first owner bought the local brickworks in 1905 when he was already living in the area with his young family. The house became the centre of a complex of offices and workers' cottages. The brickworks business was established, using the underlying high quality gault clay, as far back as the 1600s, supplying many of the grand houses in the area as well as the local parish church.

Despite the supposed free access to bricks, the owner chose the common practice of using more expensive red bricks for the visible front façade, saving a less expensive yellow colour brick for the rear, with just a single band of red stringing. The wide elaborate white painted balcony, accessed by French windows, made a statement of wealth, together with the white double storey bay sash windows. Extra embellishment was added in the form of an area of tile hanging, a band of crenellated bricks at first floor level, two square, ornamental features in relief and terracotta ridge tiles finishing with fleur-de-lis finials.

Edwardian

A word from the current owners:
When my wife and I first saw the house we both
felt immediately at home. It had a cottagey feel
and appearance, with beams, leaded-light windows
and old fashioned window catches. We liked all of
these features as well as the more quirky things –
windows that looked like a single window from the
outside but were actually split between two rooms
on the inside, level changes upstairs with two steps
up or down into a room, and a deep well outside
complete with hoisting frame and pulley wheel.
It's a great house to come home to – quiet, relaxing
and cosy.

"The mock Tudor centrepiece of
this house has a very strong presence
as it contrasts so beautifully with
the surrounding brickwork. From
an artistic point of view it's a dream
composition. The result is a powerful
drawing with strong contrasts,
especially with the L-shape (or Y-shape)
angle of the front. Beautiful…"

This house was originally built in 1909 in
the mid-Edwardian period. It portrays a
sturdy brick construction, typical of an era
when quality workmanship was held in high
esteem. The mock Tudor timber-framing and
elegant tall chimneys show the continuing
popularity of looking back to a supposedly
more picturesque time.

The interior displays exposed oak beams and wrought iron fitments. It is
appropriate that among its first residents were G K Chesterton and his family.
Chesterton was one of the luminaries of Edwardian writing circles. His most
famous books are about the detective Father Brown. Many famous visitors,
such as Walter de la Marc and George Bernard Shaw, came to visit the writer in
the beautiful setting of the Chiltern Hills.

Eli Ofir 2010

1930s

Architecture of the 1930s

Following the depression that started in America with the Wall Street Crash in 1929, the British economy improved a little in the 1930s under a National Government comprised of members from all Parties.

The late thirties were a boom time for house building in England. Houses were built to provide for an increased population brought about by new health measures. This led to higher demand for electricity, gas, water and inevitably the expansion of a workforce that served those utilities. Old industries were replaced by newer ones such as automobile and electrical manufacturers and chemical companies and a growth in agriculture was aided by new legislation that protected produce.

People wanted to own their own homes and builders tailored their designs to ensure affordability. The interwar years saw the rapid development of large areas of suburbia; the semi-detached style was predominant with each half having a similar internal floor layout.

Plumbed in kitchens and bathrooms with inside toilets were essential. With the advent of car ownership for ordinary people attached garages were increasingly becoming standard. Many style influences continued from the 1920s, or even from Edwardian houses, but mostly on a smaller scale.

At a time of financial instability and with the approach of war there was a desire for escapism. Prompted by the Paris Exhibition of 1925 and the Bauhaus style from Europe, the Art Deco and Moderne style was applied to many art forms, including architecture. It focussed on streamlined settings and avoided excessive ornamentation.

Some houses in the Moderne style featured wraparound suntrap windows or incorporated Art Deco features. Art Deco started initially with rounded motifs, such as foliage and flowers, but later became more abstract and geometric. The sunray image was especially popular and appeared in stained window glass on front doors or as top panels in front windows.

Glaswegian-born Charles Rennie Mackintosh was the driving force behind Art Deco design and architecture. Bold colours were used such as black, white and silver, often with a light-reflective finish. The look also encompassed Cubism (with zigzags and geometrics), Ancient Egyptian design (following the discovery of the tomb of Tutankhamun in 1922) and Aztec and Mayan art.

It was a new machine age style that used the innovations of the times such as plastics, chrome and aluminium. The interiors of houses were open plan with stark white painted walls and, typically, black and white chequerboard floor tiles.

Bungalows

The bungalow was a new innovation with all rooms either on a single level or, in the case of chalet style bungalows, with one or two bedrooms in the roof.

The bungalow was an ideal design for holiday homes on the coast, with flat roofs, metal windows and white finished exteriors. Here décor was likely to be softer, using ice cream colours such as pink, peach, pale green and blue or beige. Sunbathing was a new fashion and families built pergolas and balconies as suntraps.

In contrast, the mock-Tudor, Jacobean or Cottage, was an equally popular style that imitated the Arts and Crafts movement for traditional romance and decoration. House exteriors were half timbered with a mix of brick and pebbledash, or even had tile hung walls.

Windows had wooden frames with iron casements and diamond shaped leaded panes. Two storey bay windows had square or rounded sides and French windows were a common addition at the rear of houses. Doors with iron nails and fittings imitated old heavy oak examples. Red clay tiles were used on the roof rather than slate and chimney stacks were frequently elaborate. The theme continued into the interior décor where wooden parquet flooring was common.

Most of the houses from this era have survived the test of time and are considered a solid investment for family living. Although interiors have been modernised for the technological age, the streets of 1930s housing present a picture from a less complicated time.

J.D.

1930s

A word from the current owner:
I fell in love with the house the moment I saw the estate agent's details. When they arrived in the post I said: "That's it, that's our house." My husband was a bit more pragmatic, suggesting we actually visited the property before putting in an offer, but I just knew it was the house for us. Thinking about it now, I'm not sure if it was the Mediterranean look and feel of the house's exterior, with its white rendered walls and red tiled roof, or its position on a hill overlooking the North Downs Way that clinched it for me.

The house was featured in a 1925 issue of Country Life magazine and, while it has developed and expanded over the years, it still retains much of its original floor plan. The day we moved in my husband said: "This is the last home I'm buying in Britain. I feel like I'm on holiday." Seven years later our feelings haven't changed.

"A white house always brings out the beauty in a black and white hand drawn portrait, and this is no exception. I love the two huge chimneys; they are so dominant and make the house seem strong and grounded. I love the roof tiles too…"

Designed by East Anglian, Arts and Crafts architect Basil Oliver and built in 1923, this house is a classic example of his style. Oliver started his practice during the Edwardian era when this design of architecture was at its most popular and continued to use it throughout his career.
Typical features here are white rendered exterior surfaces (walls and chimneys) and a long sweeping roof. The iron railings around the balcony employed the art of a skilled blacksmith. The red glazed concrete tiled roof became more widespread in the 1930s together with the vertical band of small windows.

1930s

"The pillar to the right of the house gives the portrait magnificent composition as it stands there guarding the entrance to the park. The property seems to me like it was a gate house of some huge urban manor house. I love the contrast between the clean white house with its stained glass windows and the brick pillar."

This style of house can be found in hundreds of suburban streets and is typical of many built between the wars. A mixture of detached and semi-detached versions guaranteed that a certain amount of variety was included in the development. The white painted brickwork is reminiscent of the seaside – a frequent theme of that time.

Two-storey bay windows, some with stained glass features, were especially fashionable. The tile-covered porch with white painted woodwork frame accentuates the front door. The addition of a garage shows the increasing affluence of the first owners who probably commuted into London using the local expanding rail network. Pockets of green in the shape of golf courses and woods, together with plenty of local shops, ensure the surrounding area is both convenient and pleasant to live in. The fact that most of these houses survive in good condition speaks volumes for the original quality of construction and the continual updating by successive owners.

Thank you

I would like to thank the following people for their help and contribution to my journey that led up to the creation of this book:

- To my beloved wife Tal. Without you I would not be where I am today. Thank you for your unconditional love and for being my sole partner for life. I cherish your wisdom and insights that inspire me. Thank you for all your involvement with this book. Your beautiful design ideas and tender eye-opening remarks that awakened me for change. I feel so privileged to have you as my wife, friend, and the mother of my children. I love you deeply.

- To my parents, my mum Joyce Fisch and my late father Harold Fisch. Thank you so much for supporting my art as a child. Mum, you showed me that it is never too late to be an artist. You have huge dignity, courage and you see the good in everything. You are an inspiration to us all. I love you.

- To Yossi Harel-Fisch, my brother and his partner Lea. Thank you for being there beside me from the start and during all the most challenging times. I will never forget your devotion and I will always love you deeply.

- To my beloved daughters Noa and Yuval. You are my pride and joy and I love you for what you are. I thank you so much for all the happiness and light you bring to my life.

- To Ruth Polden, my dear friend. Thank you for all your help and the brainstorming sessions we've had. It helped me to figure out the real essence of this book.

- To Rosalind Chislett and Jane Davidson for the most professional and thorough research and investigation process. Thank you for your patience and for adding depth and academic richness to this book.

- To Neil del Strother, thank you mate for all your help with editing this book and being such a good friend.

- To the house owners who helped me create this book and who offered their lovely homes and stories. I hope I've done justice to your homes and that they are well presented. I feel a deep connection to each house and I thank you for your cooperation.

- To all my clients in England, thank you for commissioning me to draw your homes and enabling me to bring my gift to life.

Thank you all from the bottom of my heart

Eli Ofir